Mighty Machines

Military Helicopters

by Matt Doeden

Consulting Editor: Gail Saunders-Smith, PhD

Capstone
press

Mankato, Minnesota

Pebble Plus is published by Capstone Press,
151 Good Counsel Drive, P.O. Box 669, Mankato, Minnesota 56002.
www.capstonepress.com

1 2 3 4 5 6 10 09 08 07 06 05

Library of Congress Cataloging-in-Publication Data
Doeden, Matt.
    Military helicopters / by Matt Doeden.
    p. cm.—(Pebble plus: mighty machines)
    Includes bibliographical references and index.
    ISBN 0-7368-3658-6 (hardcover)
    ISBN 0-7368-5140-2 (paperback)
    1. Military helicopters—Juvenile literature. I. Title. II. Series.
UG1230.D64 2005
623.74'6047—dc22   2004012656

Summary: Simple text and photographs present military helicopters, their parts, and their crews.

Editorial Credits
Martha E. H. Rustad, editor; Molly Nei, set designer; Kate Opseth and Ted Willams, book designers;
    Jo Miller, photo researcher; Scott Thoms, photo editor

Photo Credits
DVIC, 8–9, 10–11; A1C J. S. Smorto, 7; TSGT Cesar Rodriguez, 1
Ted Carlson/Fotodynamics, cover, 5, 12–13, 14–15, 16–17, 19, 20–21

Note to Parents and Teachers

The Mighty Machines set supports national standards related to science, technology, and society. This book describes and illustrates military helicopters. The images support early readers in understanding the text. The repetition of words and phrases helps early readers learn new words. This book also introduces early readers to subject-specific vocabulary words, which are defined in the Glossary section. Early readers may need assistance to read some words and to use the Table of Contents, Glossary, Read More, Internet Sites, and Index sections of the book.

Table of Contents

What Are Military Helicopters?

Military helicopters carry
troops and supplies
to battles. Some helicopters
fight in battles.

Parts of Military Helicopters

The main rotor sits on top of a helicopter. A rotor is a set of spinning blades.

main rotor

7

The main rotor spins fast
to lift a helicopter
into the air.

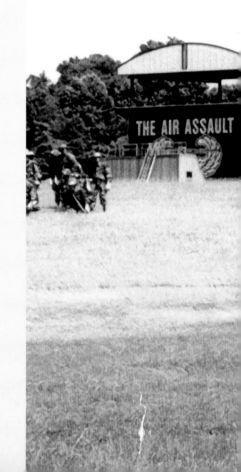

The tail rotor is at the back
of a helicopter. It helps
a helicopter turn.

tail rotor

11

Some helicopters carry guns
and missiles for fighting.

missile

gun

Some helicopters have metal armor. The armor protects helicopters from bullets.

Crews

Helicopter crews work together.

Pilots fly helicopters.

Copilots help pilots.

KY-100 BYPASS

17

Copilots or gunners shoot

guns and missiles

from helicopters.

Mighty Machines

Troops ride to battles
in helicopters.
Military helicopters
are mighty machines.

Glossary

armor—a metal covering on the outside of some military helicopters; armor protects a helicopter from bullets.

blade—the long, thin part of a rotor

crew—a team of people who work together

gunner—a crew member who shoots a helicopter's guns or missiles

missile—a weapon that flies and blows up when it hits a target; copilots or gunners aim missiles at targets, such as enemy planes.

pilot—a person who flies aircraft

rotor—a set of spinning blades; the main rotor helps lift a helicopter.

supply—an item people need to do a job; helicopters carry supplies, such as food, guns, and tents, for troops.

troops—a group of soldiers

Read More

Baysura, Kelly. *Helicopters.* Flying Machines. Vero Beach, Fla.: Rourke, 2001.

Budd, E. S. *Military Helicopters.* Military Machines at Work. Chanhassen, Minn.: Child's World, 2002.

Zuehlke, Jeffrey. *Helicopters.* Pull-Ahead Books. Minneapolis: Lerner, 2005.

Internet Sites

FactHound offers a safe, fun way to find Internet sites related to this book. All of the sites on FactHound have been researched by our staff.

Here's how:

1. Visit *www.facthound.com*

2. Type in this special code **0736836586** for age-appropriate sites. Or enter a search word related to this book for a more general search.

3. Click on the **Fetch It** button.

FactHound will fetch the best sites for you!

Index

Word Count: 106
Grade: 1
Early-Intervention Level: 16